#AliveLikeALoadedGun

~ the *mystique* of Lyn Lifshin ~

Transcendent Zero Press
Houston, Texas

PUBLISHED BY TRANSCENDENT ZERO PRESS
www.transcendentzeropress.org

ISBN-13: 978-0692729953

ISBN-10: 069272995X

Printed in the United States of America

Library of Congress Control Number: 2016943348

Cover design by AJ Price Design
Proofreading by Z. M. Wise

FIRST EDITION
Transcendent Zero Press

#AliveLikeALoadedGun

~ the *mystique* of Lyn Lifshin ~

EDITOR'S NOTE

This collection of poems was taken from separate .doc files sent to me by the author. Several poems in the files were repeated, written both in poetry form and as prose poems.

I whittled away at all the files until I decided on the collection you have in your hands. For the "Leda" section, I chose to use both versions of some of the writings to capture a feeling of being lost in a dream, as the poems themselves often reflect. The idea was to give a sense of dream images being scattered and reassembled in the ordering of the poems.

Dustin Pickering, Editor

TABLE OF CONTENTS

Opening Poems

WHEN I WILL BE SPANISH AGAIN

so long after I'm that plump girl shivering
in thin cotton my mother dyed red for
Halloween parade up Main Street, I order
"Spanish Lady" sexy adult xs on line.
Twenty years almost since her death, my
mother haunts me, I can hear her mumbling,
mouth full of pins, hemming the ruby red
cotton. I hated how my body swelled
under the tight cloth. Clearing out her apart-
ment I looked for dyed shreds, a remnant of
the dark mantilla. Too plump then, I would
not have wanted my legs exposed tho
I dreamt about a ballerina costume. Long
enough since to have children who have
children of their own, I decide Halloween
has to be Spanish. It's July and who knows
what will happen tomorrow, forget months
later but I go for the Spanish babe dress,
"very short," a customer writes for comments.
I go ahead. At least now tho my hair is no
longer night color but blonde-- I probably
will buy a wig-- my skin, ivory and taut
then now under black lace and my legs still
make me turn. Last week a man stopped
me on the metro to say they were perfect.
I couldn't help but smile. When I squeeze into
the costume's scarlet silk covered with black
lace, try to pin the comb and flimsy mantilla
into my hair I will think of my mother's fingers
behind me in the Heywood Wakefield mirror
I now have in my house, arranging and touch-
ing hair she always wanted out of my face,
so thick beauty parlors thinned it out, long
dark hair I could use now for this costume, hair
my mother always said I ruined when I dyed
and straightened it. I will remember her fingers
straightening the cotton that could never make

me look thin. My new costume has a pretty
low back, lace gloves to the shoulder, glitter,
jewels. I won't have the pink rimmed glasses I
hated and wore until college. I'll think of how
my mother would stay up, wild to hear how
things went. She'd be there if I had a good
time or came back in tears, assuring me, tho
I never believed it, I was a beauty

SHE WANTED SOMETHING

a plant that would
grow without
water, survive
ice, more
fierce than
his eyes. Her own,
needed care.
She said
who knows what
this thing called
love is, always in
mourning,
worrying her
tears will
dilute
the medicine
form her eyes

WHY SNARKY MEANS POEMS ARE DE RIGEUR

when someone's sucked
passion out of you
without even touching
you. When the dead
seem to have a more
fascinating life after
he's worn you down
for years. No matter,
it wasn't always like
this: when you can't
seem to help becoming
what you are called,
what you've called
sickens you. Forget
"living well is the best
revenge," you can't
if he is haunting you.
Just hope you have
the words to rip that
self satisfied, fake
mark from his skull,
hope that he can see
what you see in him,
it makes it feel as
he's maimed you

HOW IT CAN CHANGE

not always but
sometime what
would not bend
starts to like the
wounded Iraqi
vet, leg blown
to the other side
of the desert.
His reprieve in
dreams, the way
music moves
in thru my skin
and the floor
kisses my ballet
slippers back.
For a heartbeat
I can balance
as I used to,
finally hold a
part of me
already gone like
a cooling body
or an animal
you hold close
against you
for the last warmth

WATCHING HER BEAUTIFUL ARMS

when something so terrifying
happens to someone younger,
there is no way to describe
how perfect, still, her skin is.
Before any knives or scars.
She won't talk about it.
The V between her breasts,
lower, more plunging than
any burgundy silk or lace I've
seen her in. Outside, children
splash in the pool. From
somewhere, *I've got you under*
my skin and her mouth twitches.
Somewhere else, ravens
circle and dive. Horses move
into shade. Tonight she
will lie with her cats coiled
into the warmth of her
body as bamboo moves in
an invisible wind

ALIVE LIKE A LOADED GUN

on a night the mares
have their heads on
the ground. Bricks
suck heat in deeper.
Lavender walls,
already many dusky
shades of mauve.
Where is the girl who
leaped into Otter
Falls, a pearl of a girl
growing inside?
And the young beauty
who turned churlish
and strange? With
her turtles and rage?
Where a mother
danced in a full skirt,
kicked her legs to
Russian balalaika?
Now immaculate
polished wood and
glass turn the rooms
ice. The heart
of the house lies
open thru thick dust
on the sky light,
and a pale sun

NOT QUITE SPRING

Baby, you know I get high
on you, come back with me
whispering in her ear.
It was all she could do to say
no, spring leaves budding,
his hand on her breast,
crocus smell and
everything unfolding.
She gasping *I want, I*
would but instead hurrying
back to the windowless room
where she locks the heavy door.
Lemons are rotting on her pillow,
she studies her nipples,
nyloned crotch in mirror
then hugs her huge body to sleep

WHITE TREES IN THE DISTANCE

a white wind of
petals, maybe snow.
The longest I've
been so close to
you on the sheet
of paper. Like your
death, these poems
about you, a wild
surprise. The last
page in the note
book, still I think
I'll need another
notebook before I
can let you go

WITH STRESS, CUTS AND SORES DON'T HEAL QUICKLY

keep your tongue
in your mouth
I want to say to
everyone except
the one who does
I've had it with
lovers full of
wanna and gonna
of feeling like
some dead deer
staked on your
fender, splayed,
caught and gutted,
my head cut from
the rest, mounted,
your souvenir

HE SAYS LATELY IT'S NOT THE SAME, HARDLY WILD

the chase isn't the same,
it's like being married.
The zebras are just
trucked to you. What's

the fun without a chase,
without challenge and
danger. How can it
count if you don't have

to sweat and risk to
devour what you're
starved for. Safaris
aren't safaris these days,

more like a glop of oat
meal when you're longing
for steak, something
full of blood you can

sink your teeth in,
almost feel your whole
body in the skin of

The Ice Maiden

Peru's Ampato Ice Maiden is the first frozen Incan female mummy, and her body may be the best preserved of any found in the Americas from pre-Colombian times. Believed to be 500 years old, the mummy was discovered near the summit of 20, 700 foot Mount Ampato in the Peruvian Andes. A girl of about 12-13 years of age, she was probably offered as a sacrifice by Incan priests.

THE ICE MAIDEN'S 232nd S.O.S.

You wouldn't think that,
buried so long,
I could even respond again.
That I could hear sleet,
the branches over me
creaking and splintering.
Sometimes, I imagine
sun and light leaking through stone
that was a dream.
Then it was over.
I can't tell you how
I left what was my world for so long,
and that the first glimpse of sky
seemed like water,
my body like a pleated skirt
pressed under granite,
dark as violets,
rigid as bark,
terrified as I fell through ice crystals,
still as ice crystals,
seeing flesh and fingers
before I could feel them.

THE ICE MAIDEN'S 267TH S.O.S.

I'm a teenager,
true,
but I've been one
for 500 years,
and the further I get
from the last day,
the more I see my mother
more clearly.
How really,
there was nothing that she could do
as a woman to save me.
The weak always lie,
too terrified to say what's true.
She gave her dearest gift,
was left with nothing.
Maybe she thought it was a test,
asked to sacrifice
a daughter like Abraham and Isaac.
I thought that I might find her
under the earth,
another myth.
Don't call me Persephone.
There was no Demeter,
no Zeus.

No nothing.

Whatever I hoped,
I never found in that garden.
I was as foolish as someone
who believes that something
will grow from planting a
dead child in the ground.

WANT HAIR—
THE ICE MAIDEN'S BLUES

It begs for your fingers,
even through glass.
Don't lean too close,
the sign says, as if the iced mummy
could contaminate you,
while it's the other way around.
Once I had eggshell skin
that they sacrificed even before
I needed what you now call a Tampax.
In my village,
we braided cocoa leaves
between our thighs,
or we were called the red-legged women.
Red's always been a favorite color in my town.
See how it glistens
through the weave of my wrap.
I've want hair,
people still murmur.
I read lips through
the fog of my refrigerated case.
It's what I most was,
what I most wanted to fill
with night's jasmine, and the sounds of Java birds.
My hair never frizzed in the jungle,
or dried out at Cuzco.
Sometimes I dream it's my mother's hair,
unbound,
as she never was,
flowing and free,
revolutionary as it would have been
for her to save me.
You can see your own face
in the shine of my onyx locks.
I used to wonder if the man
who smashed my head into the rocks
first saw his eyes in that black mirror,

if he could smell the apricots
I washed it with,
if, like a body falling into the river,
his own face crumbled with mine.

THE ICE MAIDEN MUMMY'S 78TH SOS

Don't believe what you
read in the signs near
my upturned face about
my being a sacrifice but
probably dead before I
was buried in snow.
All that is true is that,
yes, it was before the
Industrial Revolution.
There were no phones.
We passed no waterfalls
on the way up the hill.
Or if there were, I
didn't see them. After
they slashed my skull,
there were no ghosts to
keep me company but
moonlight, no chit chat,
no lilac wind. No wine
dark lips moving over
me. The darkening
vowels were my dream
of an ocean, the leaves
brushing a last sentence
south until they sounded
like the sea or the moth
I was merging with fire

THE ICE MAIDEN MUMMY'S 234TH SOS

You wouldn't think
buried so long, I
could even respond
again. I could hear
sleet, the branches
over me creaking and
splintering. Then
it was quiet. Some
times I imagined sun
and light leaking
thru stone that was
a dream. Then it was
over. I can't tell
you how I left what
was my world for so
long but the first
glimpse of sky seemed
like water, my body
a pleated skirt
pressed under granite
dark as violets, rigid
as bark, terrified as
I fell thru ice crystals,
still as ice crystals,
seeing flesh and fingers
before I could feel them

THE ICE MAIDEN'S 24TH S.O.S.

Some small girls write me notes,
shove them under the base of this case
I'm caught in.
They give me a barrette,
a ribbon from their own hair,
still warm.
They say they love my long black hair,
could imagine me as a ballerina.
These are the gifts I still can adore,
their smiles and sweet breath,
as innocent as I was.
As for jewelry, fine clothes,
please.
Leave them for others.
I was given many things that
I couldn't use, gold—
they pretended I'd need them for my "journey,"
as much a lie as the words
exchanged by lovers they might
think they mean as they
kneel under a canopy
as if planting a garden they will
still be together to see it bloom.

THE ICE MAIDEN'S 27TH S.O.S.

This July, I listen to birds
in back of glass like your poet,
Emily Dickinson,
sealed off but content really
in my glass encased room.
Listening, watching.
Most of you are dashing off
to holiday events,
have your jobs,
plunge ahead.
Like the bones of the dead
in the killing fields of Bosnia,
I am not impatient.

I have plenty of time.

Sometimes I hide out
in my thick hunks of black hair,
not wanting anyone to look into my eyes.
How self-centered.
When you look deeply
into me,
I know that you are looking for yourself.
My glass cage reflects
your eyes,
the blue of wet chicory,
or glazed mahogany.

You never imagine my voice
as anything except a part of you,
whispering a warning.

THE ICE MAIDEN'S 29TH S.O.S.

Some of you think of
me as a wild her
or flower at the mercy
of light and sun,
rotted in darkness,
picked up by accident
with no will of my own.
Wind blown,
ravaged by birds,
burned or cut down,
struck by lightning.
Solitary.
True, I've been exposed,
abandoned,
but how few women
have been so treasured,
not in spite of their being
around so long,
but because of it.
My life has been a circle.
All I need is earth,
a quilt of sky.

THE ICE MAIDEN'S 77TH S.O.S.

It's not the sun that I missed,
or wanted to bathe me when
I left what I thought would
be my last room in the earth.
That was heat-pleated,
exposed, turned what
the dark held so well into leather.
No, it was the moon that
I wanted to wash over me,
silver and pale,
camouflaging my scars and wrinkles,
cool and like an opal,
mysterious enough to make of
what shimmers all that I needed.

THE ICE MAIDEN'S 79TH S.O.S.

You say that I can't sue,
a joke I guess since
I'd be grateful for the president
asking what others accuse him
of asking for.
My mouth open,
my head tilted,
really I won't say,
"give me a break."
I've already had that.
You can see how my skull
is smashed in,
my eyes that everyone said
were so pretty can't focus,
go off in different sides.
So for me,
a bolt of flesh wouldn't be worse
than ice crystals clotting
down my throat.
I need so little in comparison
to other women.
This 500 year old red dress
is still beautiful,
my teeth don't need to work.
Why should I sue?
I look up,
I have no choice,
likescilla I'm small,
but I am perennial,
go where I'm sent.

THE ICE MAIDEN'S 87TH S.O.S.

It was like being buried
though I don't remember that either.
There were the years in darkness,
and then,
it was like falling through space,
hardly thinking of the place
that I was torn from.

Later, voices were as foreign
as the words of roots
moving under the earth.

Like the first time,
I was dazed,
still frozen.
I hardly felt the stones
I slammed against,
or the sun turning my face mahogany.

By the time I was carried from
the valley, my hair smelled of
cold clover,
something was thawing,
something was at risk.

THE ICE MAIDEN'S 97TH S.O.S.

When I was born,
my mother said there
was a birthmark in the
shape of a tear,
an omen,
a warning.
But what could a
woman 500 years ago
in Peru do?
Soon this long, black hair
that many cherish,
covered it.
Still, when she held me,
she said that she held sadness,
as if she knew that
she would never have
a truce with herself,
as if the mark
was a tattoo of loss.
I hardly remember the smell,
though I rode many years
close to her skin.
When they took me to be
sacrificed to the mountain,
she didn't follow all the way,
or even come,
but she ran,
pure terror and rage:
How else could she let go
of all that mattered?

THE ICE MAIDEN'S 127TH S.O.S.

I am closer to you than I would have
expected, though you find me strangely quiet,
apart behind glass.

Listen, I didn't expect to come back to
feel light again on my fingers.
My hair trailed under roots 500 years.
Even the spiders and worms didn't outlast me.

It's hard to remember how to open.

Sometimes, I complain like some women,
even today in Japan. I'm more modest.
I can't imagine showing my breasts.

I feel gawked at.

I like the five minute limit anyone can
stare me down. But I'm grateful that so
many still find me to be a beauty.
I'm a teenager, and I often say the wrong thing.

I'm in awe at so much.

The moon glittering through the museum
skylight seems a jewel, and the closeness
of the birds, everything that I could
never hear in the other world.

THE ICE MAIDEN'S 214TH S.O.S.

It was a risk,
but everything
was after that
first death.
Terror was
suspended as
my lips were
in ice.
I didn't think
that I could
respond, or care.
I didn't expect
to open,
or feel anything
but the
Darkness.
I didn't expect
anything but
water.
I remembered
the blue iris,
the melon-colored
lilies like
someone in the
death camps
going over a
violin sonata.
I tried to
imagine my sister,
old,
in our last home,
her eyes once
like mine,
full of earth
after 500 years.
If I could choose
light, the raw wind

under the volcano
on my own,
I don't think
I would have.

THE ICE MAIDEN'S 217TH S.O.S.

Consider me.
I know that though I am
well preserved, I'm out of shape.
But if you could see my feet—
everyone tries to
once they've gazed at my
still neatly preserved shoes.
From my teeth,
you could guess that
I have strong bones.
I'm petite,
less than 80 pounds.
If a man near 50 could carry me
over his shoulder,
every part of me crystallized ice,
think on how I could leap,
no longer a dead weight.
My hair already in a ballet bun,
and like the woman in the song,
I "would never let you
see my heart breaking."
With a little sun,
my toes will be as leathery
as my face,
all the better to stand on pointe,
then to make what is torture seem effortless,
something I've done
for 500 years.

THE ICE MAIDEN'S 224TH S.O.S.

Sometimes I imagine
that I am the one who is
looking as if the streams
pouring by the case were
television images no one
can catch on video or replay.
You entertain me,
are as strange and mysterious
to me as I've heard you say
my black hair is,
my lips open,
about to gulp or howl at something
that you try to pull out of me
about my last of 500 years.
I try to lip read.
Sometimes I hear Spanish,
the language I know.
I read the lines around the woman
who feels it's easier to just stop talking.
I know a lot about this.
Since we don't talk,
I can make you up as I choose,
much as I pull back the smell of desert roses,
the Peruvian lilies that used to
twist up the hill behind my adobe house
that mother hung daisies in.
Sometimes, I see a face,
dusky as hers,
and I want to sing the lullaby that
she taught me,
only my lips are leather,
and I know that she's not here,
that she cannot hear.

THE ICE MAIDEN'S 232ND S.O.S.

You wouldn't think that,
buried so long,
I could even respond again.
That I could hear sleet,
the branches over me
creaking and splintering.
Sometimes, I imagine
sun and light leaking through stone
that was a dream.
Then it was over.
I can't tell you how
I left what was my world for so long,
and that the first glimpse of sky
seemed like water,
my body like a pleated skirt
pressed under granite,
dark as violets,
rigid as bark,
terrified as I fell through ice crystals,
still as ice crystals,
seeing flesh and fingers
before I could feel them.

THE ICE MAIDEN'S 267TH S.O.S.

I'm a teenager,
true,
but I've been one
for 500 years,
and the further I get
from the last day,
the more I see my mother
more clearly.
How really,
there was nothing that she could do
as a woman to save me.
The weak always lie,
too terrified to say what's true.
She gave her dearest gift,
was left with nothing.
Maybe she thought it was a test,
asked to sacrifice
a daughter like Abraham and Isaac.
I thought that I might find her
under the earth,
another myth.
Don't call me Persephone.
There was no Demeter,
no Zeus.

No nothing.

Whatever I hoped,
I never found in that garden.
I was as foolish as someone
who believes that something
will grow from planting a
dead child in the ground.

THE ICE MAIDEN'S 279TH S.O.S.

This is how you live
when your lips and heart are frozen,
as mine were in darkness.
My hair loose over pebbles.
I was deeper away
than anybody dreamed.
Light never touched me.
I forgot the taste of sun on my skin.
When I tried to listen
to the roots uncurl,
they became my upside-down
trees and branches.
It was like listening to someone's
teeth hit a clay jar
somewhere further than any moon.
I thought of my bones as buried silver
that explorers would unearth,
my hair a lake of onyx,
something that you wouldn't expect
to survive,
waking up,
wanting to explode into blossom.

THE ICE MAIDEN ON AN ESPECIALLY
HOT, MUGGY, D.C. DAY

Her neck aching
from the awkward way
she's propped up in
the cage at National Geographic,
she feels grumpy, used.
Blonde Ice she hisses inside
her flesh dress,
hearing of a man so in love with Barbies,
he steals 50 in a shopping cart,
and zig-zags through lines
of traffic to escape
with his love.
Not that she'd want to be
put there in the hot light.
She's already had some
bouts of melting,
feels bacteria creep in
deeper than the blues,
and after what she's been through,
hopscotching through traffic
is not on her list of top wishes.
Buckled to a llama,
knowing she was about to be murdered
was bad enough,
and then being hurled from the hole
that she finally thought of as home,
catapulted down sheer cliffs
when lava melted the ceiling.
Then,
piggy-backing down
the rest of the slope with
a man with the runs was
not her idea of a
romantic interlude
after 500 years alone,
crouched and frozen.

A kinder, gentler night,
a ride with a little soft music
would have been nice.
She knows that it's
useless to complain,

 but just because she's been on ice
for 500 years
doesn't mean that she doesn't have feelings.
And unlike
any blonde bimbo,
easily duplicated,
so promiscuous that
she's in a million bedrooms
at one time,
Juanita is unique—
she whispers through mist
in her glass case.
Barbie maybe be popular,
but she's only been around
for 30 years or so.
She's hollow and plastic.
I have eggs and she doesn't
maybe I could have a baby.
A period far beyond her scope.
And my hair is real hair,
you'd know if you touched or smelled it.

THE ICE MAIDEN DOESN'T UNDERSTAND
WHAT IT IS WITH SO MANY BLONDES

Icier than she is,
these long-legged, tall beauties
with no color.
One, a Faberge model,
found dead at 41,
a fraction of the years that I am.
And she looked so sturdy,
athletic and strong,
beautiful as a queen,
her name as pretty as mine—
Margeaux—
it sounds like May,
sounds like Myrrh,
the name of someone who'd
go on a long time.
Someone who could fight back,
sting.
Even old women with canes
in this country are blonde,
hair bleached so often that
at times,
it looks to me more than fuzz.
No wonder they mention
my long, glossy ponytail.
No one has straightened, or ironed,
or used rollers on mine,
but look how good fur kept in storage—
it looks new,
a strong, dark licorice rope
that I could let out a window
for someone to shimmy up.
And it would support me
if I could climb down to a
new life.

THE ICE MAIDEN FEELS ACHY, THE FLU, THE DAMPNESS, THE PAIN IN HER ANKLE

She knows that she ought to be grateful,
at 500 years,
who wouldn't feel a little creaky,
a little sore and cold?
Who wouldn't expect that?
With all of the strangers crowding against her,
even with glass,
she can feel their germs,
or at least thinks that she can.
And the extremes in the temperature—
when I lay on the mountain,
my body ice crystals,
sun licked my face so hot
that it dried my cheeks to leathery graves,
and no matter what the advertisements say,
nothing can fix skin so tough and hard.
But then, how many even have their own
skin at 500?
I've never had anything seriously wrong,
no tumors.
They say that I still have my eggs,
and I know from the lonely blues that my heart is still there,
still working.
Like a work of art,
kind of,
time cannot alter me that much.
My breasts are full of ice, don't droop.
I couldn't advise you to touch me, though.
Just take my word.
I don't want any sex offenders getting ideas,
thinking that just because I don't talk
that I'm fair game.
I don't even like the idea of a doctor
pummeling, prodding, and probing—
I know that it seems to be popular these days,
but it just reminds me of the way

the men who sacrificed me—
a nice word for murder—
tried to ram drugs into my throat,
and one tried to stick something
inside me where there was no place for it to go.
But I'm lucky.
I've still got my breasts and my hair,
more than many women can say.
I've heard whole families,
groups of women meet to talk of how to deal
with what they've lost and fear.
I wish that I'd had someone,
not just the roots of trees,
the stones,
the sand piled over me to talk to.
But sometimes,
it seems almost easier to curl away into myself,
escape with no voices or e-mails,
no taxes, no one to take anything from me.
Because after 500 years,
I have nothing left.

THE UNABOMBER DREAMS OF THE ICE MAIDEN MUMMY, A WOMAN IN A FLESH DRESS UNLIKE ANY OTHER

a woman used to sacrificing herself, used to sleeping under
stars in ice, with no one to talk to. He wants a woman
who won't make demands, is ok with icy behavior, would
not dream of computers or clocks or planes, or even know
they exist. Forget women with soft de-odorized skin, he wants

someone small, someone who can speak Spanish. *Juanita*
is the name he dreams he calls her, his ice maiden, waiting in
her flesh dress, the one she's worn 500 years. It's what is
inside her that matters he whispers but dreams she has
good teeth, all the better to survive in the trees. He

nuzzles his night stick. He's seen her open mouth but he
doesn't remember where, her black hair glistening as if she
just came out of the womb. And her womb, still virgin
after so long will be the one room he'll feel welcome in,
not a stranger, not shy. She'll know, from being drugged and

shoved into snow and whacked on the head, what it's like to
be pinned down on a hospital bed, in a crowd of rich Harvard
students, spread eagle without any control. He dreams her hair, a
pillow he can sleep on, wrap in, how he'll burn wild rose leaves
for her, hum a lullaby in Spanish, maybe teach her to read by

candlelight and because she has not spoken 500 years, she'll
under
stand his silence

THE ICE MAIDEN IS ASTONISHED TO HEAR THAT THE UNABOMBER LOVED CONRAD'S *SECRET AGENT*

It's not that she's read it herself—
English isn't her first language.
But she overheard explorers talking
about jungles and hearts of darkness,
and since her own had been plunged so long
in the black under snow,
she was sure it must be the color of burnt coal.
If anyone was a recluse,
after the blow on the back of her head,
surely I am one, she thinks.
Buried just like the turnips that
the Unabomber lived on,
or the carrots in Conrad's *Secret Agent*.
She thinks how similar a Montana shanty is
to a tomb that the earth's gnawed at for 500 years.
Like Theodore, she thinks, I have my own nickname.
Nobody really knows my first name,
but they call me Juanita,
or more often,
the Ice Maiden.
I know as many mysteries as any secret agents.
If Ted would just write back to me.
Who could be more alienated and lonesome than I am?
And he knows that the limelight only
makes it worse.
Science found us both out,
keeps trying to find our secrets.
Some say that I shouldn't
bitch about technology.
All of this temperature control
is keeping me from falling apart.
But the snow and ice held me longer
than your country has existed.
Like all of those people
in the books that he likes,
the Unabomber and I have been alone.

I could show him a new way of life,
how it was before engineers and scientists,
before cars, or phones, or radios,
and certainly before computers,
even math,
if he'd just let me.

THE UNABOMBER'S LETTER TO THE ICE MAIDEN THAT HE WON'T SEND

I know that you've tried to reach me—
please don't.
If I were to open to someone,
it might have been you,
but I've too much baggage.
The timing was never right.
You'd have been, perhaps, my kind of woman—
innocent and pure,
a sacrifice like those baby rabbits I tried to save.

It's too late.

I read of my mother's anguish.
There is nothing I can do.
I told her that it tears me apart to hear
even a word from them.
Think of me as someone trapped
in the deepest of jungles,
my heart is darkness.

Maybe it always was.

Brilliant, but, the papers say
about the professor in Conrad's *The Secret Agent*.
They want to see me as that man,
isolated in his tiny room,
in ragged, dirty clothes,
making a bomb to destroy an observatory.
They like to play around
with how close my name is to his creator,
that he was either JozefTeodore,
orTeodoreJozefKorzeniowski.

They are wild, Juanita.

They are wild to get into my mind
as they are in yours.
I've read in the National Geographic that
they would like to remove one of your eggs.

That's science for you.
A killer.

I know that they want to know what you ate.
It's as crazy as saying that I ate turnips
because the anarchist in the novel lived on raw carrots.
I've never been more convinced that I was right,
that I am the moral one.

I am the one who stands for freedom.

If I'd been with you near Cusco,
I would not have let them murder you.
I have saved plenty of small animals.
You talk about alienation and loneliness.
But you have slept for 500 years,
listening to the roots of trees,
the earthworms mating.
You didn't have the squeals of cars and phones,
data bases,
computers that turn everyone into robots.

It's true, there is one line of Conrad's that I do like:
"explosions were his faith,
his hope, his weapons, and his shield."

Juanita.

The Celtic Bird Goddess

THE CELTIC BIRD GODDESS' WILD SONG

you'll see me in Celtic
jewels, in tapestries,
carvings. I'm there in
the most gorgeous leaves,
echoes of my feathers
are in the swirl of rivers.
When you hear the
beauty of wings, what I
touched is touched again.
I run with the horse
goddess, with the swans,
the bull, those women,
half women, half ghostly
bird, a reminder of
strength and courage.
You will find me in your
dreams some night
it begins to snow just
after a full moon, my
feathers on your deck the
first night impatiens
wilt in the freeze. Just let
what has been closed
in you open to feeling, let
intuition unfold like a
bruise blue tulip

SOME NIGHTS THE CELTIC BIRD GODDESS

moves into the house
camouflaged among
cats and geese. I think
the mist blurred her.
Of course it was a
her. Her antics never
seem threatening
but coy. Maybe she
was cold or starved.
When I think back, I
remember feathers
on the deck, how the
almonds were gnawed
before they were
ready. It could have
been the wind I
tried telling myself
but I'm sure it was the
bird goddess. I never
saw her but it's
clear the cat did,
jolting up from blue
quilts. She was more a
presence, haunting
as a dead love whose
handwriting in a
drawer of old flannel
lures and chills. I
felt her spell, eerie as
shaking out an old
quilt from Odessa and
suddenly the room's
full of snow, a
blur. Nothing was as
it was. The Celtic
bird goddess was like
mist and the moon

was hazy thru her as
if a storm was coming

THE AMBIGUOUS, THE WILD CELTIC GODDESS' FLIGHT

think of her surges,
her wildness. How
nothing can tie her
down. Forget Leda,
raped by a swan or
better yet, think how
she flew above
disaster. Let that
ambiguity be the
wings to let you
soar, the feathers on
the deck, the sound
of wings in the
wind, a language, a
code, token of
power, symbol of
women's wildness,
fascination

WHEN I THINK OF THE CELTIC WOMAN SYMBOL, OF A WOMAN PART BIRD

in lush emerald reeds.
She migrates into your
heart, your muscles,
blood. In her eyes,
you can see woman's
transitory nature,
evolving, adapting.
She urges us to dream
of our changes of
mood and heart. Jade
ferns, jade feathers.
This Celtic goddess,
her graceful ways,
her stunning beauty,
a symbol of wild
flight and then coming
home from the under-
world, astute, crafty
and clever. She takes
you down to a magical
river, feeds you
secrets of that other
world, delicacies
of mystic realms

ANOTHER CELTIC GODDESS

was born at sunrise
when a tower of flame
burst from the new
born goddess that
reached from earth
to heaven. Some say
her son was murdered,
that she sang the first
"keening" for him.
Jade leaves turned black.
Emerald trees did
a dark riff on her pain.
Winter, a pale burial
mound until life
slithers, stirs again
and the ones who
shivered and locked
their doors call for her
blessings. She pulls
light back, blesses
candles, lets the lambs
be born

ANOTHER CELTIC BIRD GODDESS

explosive as emerald
buds after grey months
of iced fog. Suddenly
the dead months and
colorless days dissolve
and there, trailing jade
and chartreuse strands
she overwhelms you.
Druids called her
queen of Oimele
meaning Eve's milk
and they celebrate
the birth and freshness
of sheep and goats.
Her wings flame,
her stories, fiery
inspiration. Her name
translates to "fiery
arrow." I think of her
hair scented with
special woods. I think
of the rowan placed
in the heart of the
first ruby flame. She is
the goddess of poetry,
the flame of inspiration.
Ferns, reeds and maple
leaves uncurl like the
fuzzy nubs of new
antlers. Look for a sign
of her blessing, for
the foot print of a goose
or swan, a sign of
amazing luck from this
goddess often called
"the flame in the
heart of all women"

WHEN THE CELTIC BIRD GODDESS BLESSES YOUR HEALTH

leaves a shape like
the footprint of a
goose or swan,
something changes
in your house.
Her feathers are
brilliant green, her
eyes are jade,
are glowing. Who
wouldn't welcome
her arrival with
those flashes
of inspiration. She
brings poetry
and heat and light,
new lambs and
goats. Who knows
what leaves and
blossoms shimmer
in her feathery
light. Who knows
the special fortunes
ahead, only that
that shape that looks
like a goat or swan
brings the stead-
fastness and loyalty
of the goose, the
swan's savage beauty

CELTIC BIRD GODDESS

I think of her with
her blue hair and
emerald eyes. Who
wouldn't want to
lure her to her house,
their arms. Who
wouldn't dream of
being kept safe and
warm under wings of
her beauty. Goddess
of healing, poetry
and roses, she is
there at every child's
birth. The patron
deity of language,
she inspired
the alphabet. Her
braids, a rope that's
a life line. Even
today many Irish
homes have a cross
in her honor for
proliferation made
from rushes as
in the old days

CANDLES AND FIRES BURNED IN HER HONOR

the Celtic goddess of
birds and trees is some
one says, a Druid's
daughter. For her
shrine, a perpetual
flame tended by
19 virgin priestesses
called daughters
of the flame. No male
was allowed near
it. These women had
nothing to do with
any man. Even their
food supplies were
brought by other women
in the nearby town. For
over a thousand
years, the sacred flame
was tended by nuns
and before that,
for who knows how
many years, it
was kept going by
priestesses who
never were in the same
room as a man

THE DARKEST OF THE DARK CELTIC BIRD WOMEN

eyes black as night
velvet. Your cat
can't tame her. You
can't keep her
hostage. Her raven
hair, a licorice
river down her
pale skin. When you
hear her toward
dawn, you can't stay
sleeping: that
click in ebony
branches before it's
light, that raspiness,
croak croaking.
She'll eat your sun.
She's starved, she's
shy and conniving.
In your arms
she will show you
even more than
you wanted to know
but probably should

ANOTHER DARK CELTIC DARLINGS,
ANOTHER BIRD GODDESSES WITH CLAWS

she'll take you to
the river in the
blackest hours of
the night and she
will feed you
onyx lemons,
leave ebony
stains along your
skin. Her cry
is distinct, no one
else's song moves
into your blood
like hers does.
When you take
her in your
arms on October
31, her wings
bring supernatural
blessings: freeze
frames of what
is ahead and
messages from
the other world

SOME NIGHTS THE CELTIC BIRD GODDESS

moves into the house
camouflaged among
cats and geese. I think
the mist blurred her.
Of course it was a
her. Her antics never
seem threatening
but coy. Maybe she
was cold or starved.
When I think back, I
remember feathers
on the deck, how the
almonds were gnawed
before they were
ready. It could have
been the wind I
tried telling myself
but I'm sure it was the
bird goddess. I never
saw her but it's
clear the cat did,
jolting up from blue
quilts. She was more a
presence, haunting
as a dead love whose
handwriting in a
drawer of old flannel
lures and chills. I
felt her spell, eerie as
shaking out an old
quilt from Odessa and
suddenly the room's
full of snow, a
blur. Nothing was as
it was. The Celtic
bird goddess was like
mist and the moon

was hazy thru her as
if a storm was coming

CELTIC GODDESS OF THE BIRDS

the swirl of her feathers,
feathery wings. You
feel the air flutter from
her. Ravens, hawks
and eagles make up
the shadow of her arms.
Sea gulls, swans,
black birds and crows
flow thru her, around
her like rare shawls from
other worlds. Her
singing puts you in a
trance. You travel to other
realms, her cries a
warning making it hard
to tell when what isn't
wasn't still a bracelet of
birds your arms and
heart were the
nest for

THE CELTIC BIRD GODDESS

her curves, graceful
as the crane, a slim
beauty. Some believe
she arose from the
fantastic Other World
along with fairies
and elves. Her eyes,
emerald, skin pale as
any sea bird darting
thru foam, delicate as
foam. Crows and
ravens braid anklets
of darkness around her
thighs. Displease her
and her eyes glower,
eagle-fierce. Peacock-
like, a symbol of
purity, she is like a
heron, mating for life,
an ouzel, small but
tenacious. Her feathers
charm and disarm,
ribbons of
feathers linked
to ancient mysteries

THE BIRD GODDESS

Totems on her
wrists, companion,
messages, embodiments
of the magic of ancient
wisdom. Feathers
on her wrists, her ankles,
she moves between
worlds of the
living, worlds of the
dead. She moves
over jade plains and
scrub bush but
earth can't tie her down.
Suddenly she's in
the ether. Some dreams
have owl like faces
on nights black
wildness rocks hearts.
Those nights,
she's winged, is
treacherous as birds of
prey. She'll tattoo
symbols of death and
regeneration in the
branches. You'll
hear her wild cry
as her arms turn wings

THE CELTIC BIRD GODDESS

under her skin, designs
and tattooed labyrinths.
You can find her face
on pottery. Small
breasted, a peaked
face and winged. A
grid- like face
with enormous eyes.
In one cosmic
myth, primordial
existence was
in the form
of a cosmic egg
which contained a
bird epiphany
who then proceeded
to create the world

ANOTHER BIRD GODDESS

her image in clay,
she is dancing
with other women
with egg shaped
bodies. In her
house, pomegranates,
the fruit of the dead.
Where new fresh
life waits in
the womb of
the divine feminine,
blossoming stems
of vegetation
sprout from her hands

ONE BIRD GODDESS

with a beaked face
and long neck
moves thru cat tails
and ferns. Blossoming
stems of vegetation
sprout from her
hands. Her body ripens.
She holds the fruit
of the dead, part of the
cycle of life.
With so many seeds,
so much abundant
life in her womb, so
many birds on
her golden crown
the feathers she
trails, are lush with
hieroglyphs, stories of
how birth comes
from mystery

CELTIC BIRD GODDESS

birds on her upraised
arms, her long neck
embellished with
symbols of birth
out of the not-
living. Some see her
with a fish, cycle
of renewal

CELTIC BIRD GODDESS

can bridge earth,
sky and water.
On some nights,
she reminds you
of scavenging death.
Then, days later,
she is the fierce
protector of
the gentle and
fecund. Her plumes
and feathers are
alluring, luring.
Sometimes when
she flashes past
you she could be
an immortal
soul taking flight

CELTIC WATER BIRD GODDESS

in her arms, you
think of death, a soft
parting, eerie. And
yet her swan like
grace, her long sinuous
neck lures you. If
she sees danger
or imagines danger,
she becomes wildly
protect. Some believe
souls live in her
talons, that she holds
the dead, all those who
died before

CELTIC BIRD GODDESS

on a funeral urn. She
holds armfuls of
apples, carrots, peas,
symbols of her
life. She scavenges
and protects,
blights even as she
insures new life.
She challenges you,
frightens you,
lifts you from despair
so you may see
the beauty of her
creation

CARRION EATING CELTIC BIRD GODDESS

in her eyes, the
glint of souls
leaving the body.
Her hair, glistening
as raven wings.
After the sky goes
pewter, it's her
shadow. Her
shawl, a design
formed by
birds in flight,
the basis of a long
lasting system
of divination.
Some days she is
gloomy. Her
voice is foreboding
but then before
it's light, she
sings sweetly as
the birds
around her
whose presence
gives joy and eases
the pain of the
sick with
her songs

CELTIC BIRD GODDESS # 277

mysterious and colorful.
Some say they have
seen her in an iron
helmet as if ready for
combat, terrifying
and inspiring. Spirals
of vegetable
designs, characteristic
Celtic metal work
cover her hips
and buttocks, her
beautiful skin. In her
dark moods, she
can foretell the future,
hold your ears closed tho
if you hear her cries
and shrieks, wild
as a raven, if you don't
want to know what
is to come.
Especially if it's evil

MORE OF THE CELTIC BIRD GODDESS

when she appears
as a swan put on
your sunscreen:
gloom will go.
Like the rivers
and lakes, all the
bodies of water
she hangs out
in, she possesses
therapeutic powers.
For the Celts,
swans morph into
humans, often
wear human jewels.
Under a finger
nail moon, this
goddess may turn
into a swan

ARIEL, THE CELTIC BIRD GODDESS

posses wild aspects:
the maiden whose
singing brings the
dawn, mother of
winds who hatches
the Cosmic Egg and
the dark winged crow
who guides spirits
of the newly dead
into heavenly after
life. She is attended
by song birds and
vultures. The bird
goddess brings
messages and omens
on wild wings from
the other world.
She covers children
with soft feathers
and sacred eggs.
Souls are weighed
against feathers.
Her keen eyes see
thru all deceptions
into the future.
Her sharp talons
and beak tear away
the gross things
in the world so
imagination can soar
free. She is the
ancient power of
flight which connects
our spirits in the
first breath of dawn

CELTIC BIRD GODDESS FROM THE UNDERWORLD

comes disguised as
a swan, often moving
between worlds,
elegant as veiled
poetry. Some nights
she's unlaced. Gold
and silver chains
circle her pale long
neck. "Supernatural,
supernatural," the
leaves sing. Gold
from the sun, silver
the moon. In dreams
the bird goddess
asks us to spread our
wings, fly into our
waking dreams

MORE OF THE SWAN BIRD GODDESS

in the white moon
when the lilies are
shuddering in
blackness. She
wants you to
cleanse and
purify our life.
Then she morphs
into darkness.
Her black feathers
glint, onyx, wild
licorice. She
wants anything in
you you don't
want to be
transformed like
ugly ducklings
into beauty

CELTIC BIRD GODDESS

some say she is
uncivilized, "kelto,"
primitive and wild.
Some say it was
from her we have
plaid, that her
multicolored
feathers
have brought
color into
our lives

CELTIC GODDESS OF THE BIRDS

wears her hair long
but shaved the rest
of her body. Naturally
light, she washes
her hair with lime,
draws it back
from her forehead
to the nape of
her neck. Some say
she looks like
satyrs or Pan, that
it is so thickened
by this treatment it
looks no different
than a horse's mane

CELTIC FERTILITY GODDESS

in sacred groves,
deep in blackly
jade forests with
dark springs. An
untrimmed tree
trunk rots to
whiteness. She'll
prepare a ritual
sacrifice under the
branches, lead
up two white bulls
whose horns are
bound for the
occasion. A Druid
in white climbs
the tree with a
pruning hook, cuts
the mistletoe
which is caught
in a white silk cloth

CELTIC WALL PLATE BIRD GODDESS

faces of gold
circled by sand
colored feathers
on a blue face
with blazing
lime eyes. The
most beautiful
oval eyes, a
come hither
smile and then
the bird woman
in a circle
within a circle
in her circle
where life
begins

RHIANNION HORSE GODDESS WITH HER BIRD

the white witch, the
great queen, she inspires
poets, artists and singers.
Wind shakes the barley.
She posses deep magic,
uses her dreams for the
good of all. She's a good
witch, a healer. She
straddles a white mare
with her mysterious birds
that possess healing powers,
can bring a child to those
told they never could

MORE OF RHIANNON THE HORSE GODDESS

the princess who lies
like a shadowy
creature in the realm
of our dreams
waiting to come to
life with vigor
and passion again.
Patient as she is
beautiful, she is also
courageous, will
make you ache to
hear her sing with
her magnificent
singing birds that
heal with their
magical voices

THE MYSTICAL FIRE BIRD GODDESS

her swirls of purples,
reds and blue hypnotize.
She is said to have
been the only living
creature allowed to fly
into Paradise. Sacred
to the sun, she lived on
the wing, having a life
span of 500 to 1000
years. Of all the
goddesses, hers is
the sweetest sound and
her tears heal. She is
a symbol of the
eternal cycle of time
and existence, the
importance of old endings
and new beginnings.
Each rebirth
is at a higher level.
She heralds that the time
has come for you to
be reborn in mind,
body and spirit, to slough
off your old life in
order to face important
new challenges. You
must not feel daunted.
She tells you so you
will rise stronger and more
beautiful from the ashes
of your old self, that
the essence of all things
in reality may be transformed

Swan and Leda

Parts I and II

THE BLACK ANGEL

came in thru Dulles
disguised as a man I
thought I knew. Of
course it was her
there was soot on her
fingers, a sheen as if
what once glowed
darkened. She left me
E Mail, a voice mail.
If I had spoken to her
maybe I'd have known.
If it was a video phone
I wouldn't have been
taken, lured to the
motel on a broken
down street in a misty
rain of ice crystals
where, because I was
so cold of course I
let what I thought was
a man, an old friend,
wrap his hands around
mine, around me was
one thing. But to follow
what I thought was
an editor to his room
and gulp wine because
I was still freezing,
pull the quilts around
me like a shawl, was not
quite the same. I caught
a glimpse of black
wings in the mirror
the angel thought I could
not see, saw evil and
danger dripping like
ashes. Leaving my

manuscript behind, hardly
carrying if I skidded thru
ice, I escape room 274,
heard her whisper *A one
kiss from me and you'll
be dead,* and I ran
faster than I thought
I could, collapsed on the orange line

THIS DECEMBER

A swan moved into the house,
camouflaged among geese.
She must have been, or
the mist from the pond
blurred her. I say her
because her antics never
seemed male. Never threatening,
but coy. And never loitering
on my side of the bed. I
suppose she was cold or starved.
This year, the pond froze early.
When I think back, I remember
a white feather on the deck
but that wasn't so strange.
The tangerines were gnawed
before they were ripe. It
could have been crows or
gulls I told myself after
the space between my lover
and I in bed got wider. He
thought this ghost bird was
lovely as he had psychotic
ballet dancer lovers who
became swans. The quilt's
full of feathers he'd insist
when a pale wreathe of her
circled the sheets. I thought
it was more like something wild
staking territory. It wasn't
that we really saw her though
it is clear the cat did. She was
more of a presence and haunting
as a dead love whose handwriting
lures and chills. I felt her
watch him. She knew his moods,
each move and had more time to
plot seduction than I did.

Being unattainable didn't hurt.
He felt her breath and his blood
couldn't sleep. Drugs hardly
helped but for once, he didn't
mind not sleeping. When he turned
up music too loud for me, she
moved into his arms downstairs.
I kept typing. I could feel her
legs sprawled open like a dancer
with a miracle 180 degree arabesque,
hardly human, a wild open grin. Crumbs
and bread disappeared. There were
more feathers, it was like a mist
and the moon was hazy through her
as if a storm was coming. Once when
I opened an old quilt from Odessa
the room filled with its snow.
Some days seemed as opaque. The
day the pond froze for good the
house felt somehow different. The cat
stopped being spooked. A downstairs
window looked splintered but then
I saw it was only frost etched
in what looked like a hieroglyph,
something in a language I don't know.
I vacuumed up the last feathers.
The stain of wings still hangs in
the air, gives the room a bluish light.
Still, her leaving wasn't like a break
up where someone leaves the house,
packs a painting, favorite gloves but
more the way something comes apart,
as it did, so slowly it's hard to
tell when what isn't wasn't still
whole

EVEN BEFORE THE POND FREEZES OVER

There were feathers,
closer and closer to
the house. Not just dark crow
wands or strands from the
wild geese but a

white that seemed tipped
with flesh. And tho this
may sound strange, a whiff
of magnolia, even in
November. At first, it was only

a feeling that someone else
was in the room, a something
loitering on the deck,
swaying against bleached wood.
The first time I

dreamed her pinched face, I didn't connect
her to the feathers but then
there were more signs. And in the
dark I heard moaning. It sounded

like another language. Then
I picked out, "Leda's child," and "Leda's
girl," over and over. I thought I was
imagining this until I found
rose velvet cluttered with feathers
near the shore

and claw marks, almost a note in the sand.
One night and I can't swear it wasn't
a dream, something half woman, half bird
seemed to be perched on the foot of the
bed, a pale woman with wings
where there'd be arms

and in the morning, the shades
looked clawed or pecked. Maybe if
I had reached out.... But it could
have been a dream and she seemed
so angry, homeless, maybe unable to find
a place she could fit in. She might have seen
us feeding the geese, somehow hoped to find
someone who could hold her

It was clear she didn't like
men. She always came to me. My
husband rarely saw her. Who could blame her
after her mother had been raped
by a swan. Maybe she was curious about
her father. Once I thought I could feel

her sleeping coiled against my hip,
starved for warmth, shoving the cat out. She
ate less than the cat, maybe feeling too earth bound
with her woman's breasts and hips, hoping for flight.
She seemed to be looking up at the sky
on the balls of her felt as if aching
to turn those feathers she'd
been cursed by into wings

EVEN BEFORE THE POND FREEZES OVER

There were feathers, closer
and closer to the house. Not
just dark crow wands or strands
from the wild geese but a
white that seemed tipped
with flesh. And tho this
may sound strange, a whiff
of magnolia, even in
November. At first, it was
only a feeling that someone
else was in the room, a some
thing loitering on the deck,
swaying against bleached wood.
The first time I dreamed her
pinched face, I didn't connect
her to the feathers but then
there were more signs. And in
the dark I heard moaning. It
sounded like another language.
Then I picked out, "Leda's child,"
and "Leda's girl," over and over.
I thought I was imagining this
until I found rose velvet cluttered
with feathers near the shore and
claw marks, almost a note in the
sand. One night and I can't swear
it wasn't a dream, something
half woman, half bird seemed
to be perched on the foot of
the bed, a pale woman with wings
where there'd be arms and in
the morning, the shades looked
clawed or pecked. Maybe if I
had reached out.... But it could
have been a dream and she seemed
so angry, homeless, maybe unable
to find a place she could fit in.

She might have seen us feeding
the geese, somehow hoped to find
someone who could hold her. It
was clear she didn't like men.
She always came to me. My
husband rarely saw her. Who
could blame her after her mother
had been raped by a swan. Maybe
she was curious about her father.
Once I thought I could feel
her sleeping coiled against my
hip, starved for warmth, shoving
the cat out. She ate less than
the cat, maybe feeling too earth
bound with her woman's breasts
and hips, hoping for flight.
She seemed to be looking up at
the sky on the balls of her felt
as if aching to turn those feathers
she'd been cursed by into angel wings

THIS DECEMBER

A swan moved into the house, camouflaged
among geese. She must have been, or the
mist from the pond blurred her. I say her
because her antics never seemed male. Never
threatening, but coy. And never loitering
on my side of the bed. I suppose she was
cold or starved. This year, the pond froze
early. When I think back, I remember a white
feather on the deck but that wasn't so strange.
The tangerines were gnawed before they were
ripe. It could have been crows or gulls I
told myself after the space between my lover
and I in bed got wider. He thought this
ghost bird was lovely as he had psychotic
ballet dancer lovers who became swans. The
quilt's full of feathers he'd insist when a
pale wreathe of her circled the sheets. I thought
it was more like something wild staking territory.
It wasn't that we really saw her though it is
clear the cat did. She was more of a presence
and haunting as a dead love whose handwriting
lures and chills. I felt her watch him. She
knew his moods, each move and had more time to
plot seduction than I did. Being unattainable
didn't hurt. He felt her breath and his blood
couldn't sleep. Drugs hardly helped but for
once, he didn't mind not sleeping. When he turned
up music too loud for me, she moved into his arms
downstairs. I kept typing. I could feel her legs
sprawled open like a dancer with a miracle 180 degree
arabesque, hardly human, a wild open grin. Crumbs
and bread disappeared. There were more feathers,
it was like a mist and the moon was hazy through her
as if a storm was coming. Once when I opened an old
quilt from Odessa the room filled with its snow.
Some days seemed as opaque. The day the pond froze
for good the house felt somehow different. The cat

stopped being spooked. A downstairs window looked
splintered but then I saw it was only frost etched
in what looked like a hieroglyph, something in a
language I don't know. I vacuumed up the last
feathers. The stain of wings still hangs in the
air, gives the room a bluish light. Still, her
leaving wasn't like a break up where someone leaves
the house, packs a painting, favorite gloves but
more the way something comes apart, as it did, so
slowly it's hard to tell when what isn't wasn't
still whole

EVEN BEFORE THE POND FROZE OVER

There were traces, even before blood
leaves fell from the oak, the feathers
began to move closer. There were always some
in the grass the mallards and wild
geese grazed in. But these were totally

white, smelling vaguely of roses. First
I thought the scent was my own skin. Or the
tea roses in the garden. But something wilder
mixed in. I could feel a shadow, even in the
brightest light, something like me but not

me. Sometimes in the mirror, I feel her pale
eyes right behind me like a daughter I never
chose. If I knew Morse code, maybe I'd have
understood the tapping on glass at night. One
morning an envelope with no postage appeared on

the stairs and handwriting I had to put up
to the mirror to read said, "Leda's daughter,"
and I thought of the feathers rising up
thicker, piling against lawn chairs on the deck
until the sun goes. I think of a woman raped

by a swan, her face white as lilies. Some
thing dissolving the way men melted, snow on
the battlefields in Fredricksburg. The
flutter of wings and claws become shadows,
the deepest black. Even now, this long later,

it flutters over the grass, wild to
soar above earth her mother was ground into,
to use the wings that used her, soar above
everything she's heard the stories of to
redefine *ravishing* and become an angel

PALE FEATHERS SNAGGED

in the sheets by late
summer and there were voices
scratching the blinds like
fingers parting what was
closed to watch for a car

from another city. The moon
wrinkled in the pond, wine
and blood ripples, eerie as
the most ordinary room in
fever, on a night with a

stranger you wake up dazed
from, bruises blooming, black
roses in too bright light
unravelling across the floor.
It was like that, the presence

of something I couldn't touch.
I don't think it was other
loses. In the dream, she was
wrapped in her own wings, said
she was Leda's daughter, how

her mother never forgot the
night of rape. How after that
she felt like stamps in the
rain gluing what shouldn't
be stuck together

and how her mother never
could hold her close with
these wings that arched
toward the sky, plotting a
way to lift up out of the

dust and the roses,
suspended like our geese
over a trail of pain
to become an angel

SHE COMES TO THE RIVER WHEN I FEED THE GEESE

part swan, part woman.
Some mornings she's
starved. She hovers
at the foot of the
bed, eats what the
birds do, eats like a
bird. Feathers drift
from her, billow
like swirling snow.
The billows I fluff
seem thinner, as if
she came, grew out of
something inside what
I hold but I know that's
not true. It was clearly
a rape. Her mother was
Leda she's told me in
the code of her foot
prints in wet grass.
A beauty, she was
ravished, the word they
used then. She was raped
and left with a baby,
part swan. Like her
mother she feels crushed,
alien. The geese shove
her aside. Her mother
couldn't hold her
feathers where there
should have been arms,
wings that made her
sneeze. The girl picked
at her food, couldn't
use a knife or spoon, or
hold the barre at ballet
though she could glide,
suspended in the air.

The bird's voices seem
like a language she almost
knows but in the end it
eludes her. She hovers,
runs along the pond like
men in films who know that
if they run fast enough
with their hand made wings
they could float up into
the wind like angels, held
in the arms of nothing

FOR MONTHS SHE CAME AT NIGHT,
A STRANGE PRESENCE

like the beating of
something flying
against the glass
or the swirl of water
in a conch shell, a
shadow of a shadow.
Then she got more bold,
could unhinge the
porch door silently,
help herself to berries
or bread. First I thought
I imagined the hole in
the muffins as if some
thing with a beak found
a way in. And then, the
trail of crumbs downstairs
out to the pond. One
morning before guava
rose over the skin of
water, it was the
second night I couldn't
sleep and wanted
at least to see sun rise
when I saw something
no body would believe
unless they believed
in angels. A woman,
mostly a woman, with
wings in the wet grass with
doves and geese. She didn't
have arms, not like a
thalidomide baby, but
more like another bird.
An angel, except for a
huge beak where the
Christmas cards have soft

lips usually smiling.
She started to move,
to walk into the water
but I beckoned, put
my hand out to her as
if nothing seemed
strange and after she
hesitated she kind
of fluttered up toward
me, her head lowered as
if she was sure I'd be afraid.
That must have been, I
realized later, what
she expected of most women.
I'm Leda's girl she
whispered cowering inside
those wings that were
like a screen I imagined
her camouflaged behind,
some Gipsy Rose Lee
doing a costume change,
coming out with a basket
of fruit on her head. "The
daughter of rape,"
she hissed, more like
the geese, getting bolder.
My mother was ravished,
raped. Without arms, I
could be Venus. Without
arms, she could have loved
me but these wings
remind her of that day
everything changed. Now
I crouch like statues
of angels in the gardens
rain and sleet pelt, earth
bound and cracked,
still dream of flight

LEDA'S GIRL

"That's what everybody calls me,"
she confided when she no longer
cowered, shrank from my gaze.
It's true, with so much about
her resembling an angel, the
beak did startle and jar. The
wings could have belonged to an
angel, feathers covering where
arms would be from her shoulders
to her calves. White as egg whites.
If I didn't look higher, I could
imagine her on some Christmas
tree, or near the sundial among
roses in the gardens at Yaddo.
Something about her was as unique
as the space you or I could make
lying in snow. But, like that
space, darkness filled her. "It
started with the rape," she told me
months after I first saw feathers
float on foam. "And everything
ended for my mother that night and
in a way, my being created was a
part of her end too. She never sang
or smiled. How could she? I'm a
daily reminder of what shoved the
light away from her face. How could
I hold her without making her shake,
remember being smothered in feathers,
forced into the marsh grass she'd
see after that as a grave, even when
I forced my way through, unable to
conceal everything about me I
couldn't help but hate

LEDA'S GIRL

"That's what everybody calls me,"
 she confided when she no longer
 cowered, shrank from my gaze.
 It's true, with so much about

 her resembling an angel, the
 beak did startle, jar. The
 wings could have belonged to an
 angel, feathers covering where

 arms would be from her shoulders...

IT MUST HAVE BEEN HER, THE BLACK ANGEL

what else could have
slammed into the
stillness, a weekend
nobody yelled and
the cat ate the first
can I opened, usually.
Then, I felt her like
something growing
inside that shouldn't.
Some tree of glass
that could tear parts
of you from yourself
as it pushed boundaries
wild for light. I felt
branches poking thru
my hips and navel,
crow fingers, a caw
of stone as she turned
my tongue onyx.
Her obsidian words
an SOS written in
black ink in a language
no one still knows
on the black river

Enheduanna

ENHEDUANNA, DAUGHTER OF AKKAD AND HIGH PRIESTESS OF THE MOON GOD NANNA IN THE SUMERIAN CITY STATE OF UR. BORN 2285 B.C. IN MESOPOTAMIA, ENHEDUANNA WAS THE FIRST PERSON, AND A POET, WHO SIGNED HER NAME TO A POEM SHE HAD WRITTEN

Educated, in love with words
before the sun was too hot
in the shade of dates and olives,
she pressed her stylus into damp
clay into cuneiform tablets,
sensual as the damp breeze
thru the reeds, lovely as the
calcite white moon shaped
disc found in several fragments
in the temple of Ningal with
her words on one side of
the limestone figure, on the
other, calm and clear eyed
Enheduanna, individualistic and
determined. Prickly acacia wind.
Enheduanna wears a long
robe of fleecy Kaunakes instead
of a shawl, three braids rest
on her breast. She wears a simple
scarf wound like a diadem
about her head with one
arm raised to let you know she
knows where she is going
and that she will get there

IN THE HEAT OF THE EUPHRATES

Enheduanna becomes used
to men listening to her,
wondering if they were
really listening to what she
said or watching her shiny
dark lips as she wrote
on her lapis lazuli tablet.
If she were alive in our rime
she'd be a feminist surely
of maybe in politics, or a
jazz singer scatting and of
course with her own blog.
As it was, I see her sitting
near the Nile using snippets
of her life as she praised
gods, goddesses often with
multiple meanings, the
saffron wind on her
shoulders, the hot dust
from the pyramids
in the juniper wind

HER HEART'S WORDS, HER WILD PASSION

The hot light turns
her breasts copper.
In a daze of the Rose
of Jericho, Enheduanna
carves her breath, her
words, chisels stone
with the fire and
passion, her love of
words. The first woman
to write her breath
and blood in her
story of creation,
she takes a deep
breath then signs her
name to the poem

MORNINGS BEFORE THE DEW DISSOLVES

and gazelles move thru acacia,
Enheduanna watches Damask
roses climbing vines before
anyone is awake. She is dreaming
of words for the day. She wanders
in a wind of blue jasmine years
before Jesus. Danger braids
with her love. Her heart a burning
river until she fills her cuneiform
with clay and lets the wild
animal in her out

SHE IS MYSTERIOUS AS

the fruit no longer growing
anywhere in Mesopotamia.
Was she secretive
behind the ambiguity
of her words? Masked?
Did she share with her
mother, the Sumerian,
her own dreams
and fears written with
gut wrenching honesty?
Did she dream her words
would last over 500
years? Was it her passion
that led some to say
"Psychological, sophisticated
insights that made her
a sheer genius and parallel
even by Shakespeare?"

WHEN SHE FELT INJUSTICE SHE WROTE

I no longer lie in the goodly place.
Today the sun scorches, and I
came to the shade of night,
the South wind overwhelming.
My honey sweet voice has become
strident. What ever gave me
pleasure has turned to dust

SOME DAYS ENHEDUANNA DRESSES IN RUBY FLAME TO RECEIVE INSPIRATION

she has heaped
up coals to
to receive poetic
inspiration, "madness"
as she calls it, "mellifluous
mouth, mourns
when her choicest
features are turned
to dust

WILD DUCKS GRAZED THE PALM TREES

near Enheduanna's window
the Tigris laps her heart beat.
She can't sleep, can't lean
into any dream or play
evening rain like a lute.
Once she dreamt her flutes
were burned and scalded,
roses smeared across
the walls but this night she
goes out in the dark
blackness to walk among
the Nakia date palms, tall,
proud and tough as she
prays she will be

SOME BELIEVE A WOMAN WANDERS THE HILLS

her spirit braids with
the Arabian desert,
with the Syria desert.
The pastoral Bedouins
feel it in their caravans
when they lie down
with camels. In the
stars, they see her
light, yellow jonquils
here and there skim
over chaos like a
river of mercury. They
believe she opens like
a June evening,
balloons like a storm
and knows you will
know it all

ENHEDUANNA TWISTS AND UNTWISTS THE TANGLES OF LIFE

she is humming a
blues riff, stories
of love and loss.
Men must have
lusted for her
thick mahogany
hair, smelling of
almonds, must
have wanted her
lips bright as coral
as she moved
thru barley
and wild dogs
she was
oblivious to

WHO'S TASTED THE END AND THE ENDLESS

like a wild winged
thing that blows
rose petals thru
windows covered
with gauze. She
is like a dancer,
Enheduanna's
feet barely touch
earth. Her words
fill with laughter,
then with sorrow

THEN SHE WRAPS YOUR HEART IN SCARLET SASHES

cuneiform still on
her fingers.
Heat leaks in
to the Tigris,
Saffron and
fragrant oil
trail from her
body to melt
moon and stars
that drip to
earth reaping
gold petals,
dandelions

YOU WERE DRINKING IN

the sweet thick
taste under the
gauzy moon.
The nectar of
death. if there
were roses
they would
dropped their
petals

SEALED IN CLAY

500 years ago
Enheduanna's
blue riff to Ioanna.
It dazes to know
her jewels were
untouched for
years and years
like a love letter
in language
no one can
decipher 6,000
years later

OTHER TRANSCENDENT ZERO PRESS TITLES

splake

t. kilgore splake

Passion's Zest

Marcie Eanes

Qualities I: Polysyllabic Motets for Performance

Richard Kostelanetz

The Ascent of Feminist Poetry and

Ends of the Earth: Collected Poems

Charles Bane, Jr.

Songs of a Dissident

Scott Thomas Outlar

A Bizarre Burning of Bees

AJ Huffman

See more *at* www.transcendentzeropress.org!

ALL TITLES ARE AVAILABLE AT AMAZON.COM

ABOUT THE AUTHOR...

Lyn Lifshin has published over 130 books and chapbooks including three from Black Sparrow Press: *Cold Comfort, Before It's Light,* and *Another Woman Who Looks Like Me.* Lifshin published her prize winning book about the short-lived beautiful race horse Ruffian, *The Licorice Daughter: My Year With Ruffian,* and *Barbaro: Beyond Brokenness.* Her recent books include *Ballroom; All the Poets Who Have Touched Me, Living and Dead; All True, Especially The Lies; Light At the End: The Jesus Poems; Katrina; Mirrors; Persephone; Lost In The Fog; Knife Edge & Absinthe: The Tango Poems.* NYQ Books published *A Girl Goes into the Woods.* Also just out: *For the Roses,* poems after Joni Mitchell, and *Hitchcock Hotel* from Danse Macabre. *Secretariat: The Red Freak, The Miracle* and *Tangled as the Alphabet– The Istanbul Poems* was just released from NightBallet Press as well *Malala,* the DVD of *Lyn Lifshin: Not Made of Glass.* The *Marilyn Poems* was just released from Rubber Boots Press. An update to her Gale Research Autobiography is out: *Lips, Blues, Blue Lace: On The Outside.* Also just out: *Femme Eterna* and *Moving Through Stained Glass: the Maple Poems.* Forthcoming: *Degas Little Dancer* and *Winter Poems* from Kind of a Hurricane Press, *Paintings and Poems* from Tangerine Press (just out) and *The Silk Road from Night Ballet.*

Learn more at www.lynlifshin.com

CPSIA information can be obtained at www.ICGtesting.com
Printed in the USA
LVOW11s1732110916

504142LV00009B/633/P